MASTERING THE GRADE 6 PSSA WRITING ASSESSMENT

– A WRITER'S WORKBOOK –

JAMES KILLORAN

STUART ZIMMER

MARK JARRETT

JARRETT PUBLISHING COMPANY

EAST COAST OFFICE
P.O. Box 1460
19 Cross Street
Ronkonkoma, NY 11779
631-981-4248

WEST COAST OFFICE
10 Folin Lane
Lafayette, CA 94549
925-906-9742

1-800-859-7679   Fax: 631-588-4722
www.jarrettpub.com

Jarrett Publishing Company
Post Office Box 1460
19 Cross Street
Ronkonkoma, New York 11779

ISBN 1-882422-64-3
Printed in the United States of America
by Malloy Lithographing, Inc., Ann Arbor, Michigan
First Edition
10 9 8 7 6 5 4 3 2 1   04 03 02 01

ACKNOWLEDGMENTS

The authors would like to thank the following educators who reviewed the manuscript. Their comments, suggestions, and recommendations proved invaluable in preparing this book.

Collin T. Wansor, Ph.D.
Writing Assessment Consultant
Hempfield Area High School
Greensburg, Pennsylvania

Joan W. Higgs (Retired)
Teaching Consultant, NCTE
Secondary English and Team Leader
Central York School District
Seven Valleys, Pennsylvania

Cover design, layout, graphics, and typesetting:
Burmar Technical Corporation, Albertson, N.Y.

This book is dedicated…

to my wife Donna, and my children Christian, Carrie, and Jesse

— James Killoran

to my wife Joan, my children Todd and Ronald, and
my grandchildren Jared and Katie

— Stuart Zimmer

to my wife Gośka, and my children Alexander and Julia

— Mark Jarrett

Other books by Killoran, Zimmer, and Jarrett
Mastering the Grade 5 PSSA Reading Test
Mastering the Grade 3 ISAT Reading and Writing Tests
Mastering the Grade 5 ISAT Reading and Writing Tests
Mastering the Grade 3 MCAS Reading Test
Mastering the Grade 4 MCAS Tests in English Language Arts
Mastering New York's Grade 4 English Language Arts Test
Mastering New York s Grade 8 English Language Arts Test
Mastering Ohio's Fourth Grade Proficiency Tests in Reading and Writing
Mastering the Grade 4 FCAT Reading and Writing Test
Mastering the Elementary English Language Arts
Introducing the Elementary English Language Arts

TABLE OF CONTENTS

INTRODUCTION
A NOTE TO STUDENTS USING THIS BOOK

Writing is an extremely complex act. It involves creating, developing, and combining ideas into sentences, paragraphs, and longer passages. The writer must consider who will read what is being written and adjust his or her style to that audience. Writing well requires the ability to shape particular messages to the intended audience, and to meet the requirements of standard written English.

The purpose of this book is to help you to improve your writing while preparing you for the **Grade 6 PSSA Writing Assessment.** You will review the basic tools of writing and learn how to analyze writing prompts like those found on the PSSA Writing Assessment.

You will also practice writing narrative, informational, and persuasive essays. In addition, you will learn about the five domains (*characteristics*) of good writing. These domains will be used to score your response. The final unit of this book contains a complete practice test similar to the **Grade 6 PSSA Writing Assessment.**

If you carefully review this book, complete the practice exercises, and pay attention to your teacher, you can feel confident that you will do your very best when the day of the actual test arrives.

PENNSYLVANIA'S ACADEMIC STANDARDS FOR WRITING

The Pennsylvania Department of Education has identified several standards or goals they want each student to have achieved by the sixth grade. The Grade 6 PSSA Writing Assessment, measures how well you have achieved these standards. Before we examine anything else, let's begin by looking at these writing standards:

Pennsylvania's public schools shall teach, challenge, and support every student to realize his or her maximum potential and to acquire the knowledge and skills needed to:

STANDARD 1.4.5

A. Write poems, plays, and multi-paragraph stories.
  - ★ Include detailed descriptions of people, places, and things.
  - ★ Use relevant illustrations.
  - ★ Utilize dialogue.
  - ★ Apply literary conflict.
  - ★ Include literary elements.
  - ★ Use literary devices.

B. Write multi-paragraph informational pieces (e.g. essays, descriptions, letters, reports, instructions).
  - ★ Include cause and effect.
  - ★ Develop a problem and solution when appropriate to the topic.
  - ★ Use relevant graphics (e.g. maps, charts, graphs, tables, illustrations, photographs).

C. Write persuasive pieces with a clearly stated position or opinion and supporting details, citing sources when needed.

STANDARD 1.5.5

A. Write with a sharp, distinct focus identifying topic, task, and audience.

B. Write using well-developed content appropriate for the topic.

 ★ Gather, organize and select the most effective information appropriate for the topic, task and audience.

 ★ Write paragraphs that have a topic sentence and supporting details.

C. Write with controlled and/or subtle organization.

 ★ Sustain a logical order within sentences and between paragraphs using meaningful transitions.

 ★ Include an identifiable introduction, body, and conclusion.

D. Write with an understanding of the stylistic aspects of composition.

 ★ Use different types and lengths of sentences.

 ★ Use precise language including adjectives, adverbs, action verbs and specific details that convey the writer's meaning.

 ★ Develop and maintain a consistent voice.

E. Revise writing to improve organization and word choice; check the logic, order of ideas and precision of vocabulary.

F. Edit writing using the conventions of language.

 ★ Spell common, frequently used words correctly.

 ★ Use capital letters correctly.

 ★ Punctuate correctly (periods, exclamation points, question marks, commas, quotation marks, apostrophes.)

 ★ Use nouns, pronouns, conjunctions, prepositions and interjections properly.

 ★ Use complete sentences (simple, compound, declarative, interrogative, exclamatory and imperative).

G. Present and/or defend written work for publication when appropriate.

THE PENNSYLVANIA WRITING ASSESSMENT SCORING GUIDE

	FOCUS	CONTENT	ORGANIZATION	STYLE	CONVENTIONS
4	Sharp, distinct controlling point made about a single topic with evident awareness of task (mode)	Substantial, specific, and/or illustrative content demonstrating strong development and sophisticated ideas	Sophisticated arrangement of content with evident and/or subtle transitions	Precise, illustrative use of a variety of words and sentence structures to create consistent writer's voice and tone appropriate to audience	Evidence control of grammar, mechanics, spelling, usage, and sentence formation
3	Apparent point made about a single topic with sufficient awareness of task (mode)	Sufficiently developed content with adequate elaboration or explanation.	Functional arrangement of content that sustains a logical order with some evidence of transitions	Generic use of a variety of words and sentence structures that may or may not create writer's voice and tone appropriate to audience	Sufficient control of grammar, mechanics, spelling, usage, and sentence formation
2	No apparent point but evidence of a specific topic	Limited content with inadequate elaboration or explanation.	Confused or inconsistent arrangement of content with or without attempts at transitions	Limited word choice and control of sentence structures that inhibit voice and tone	Limited control of grammar, mechanics, spelling, usage, and sentence formation
1	Minimal evidence of a topic	Superficial and/or minimal content	Minimal control of content arrangement	Minimal variety in word choice and minimal control of sentence structures	Minimal control of grammar, mechanics, spelling, usage, and sentence formation

NON-SCOREABLE	OFF-PROMPT
• Is illegible; i.e. includes so many indecipherable words that no sense can be made of the response • Is incoherent; i.e. words are illegible but syntax is so garbled that response makes no sense • Is insufficient; i.e. does not include enough to assess domains adequately • Is a blank paper.	• Is readable, but did not respond to prompt

Unit 1:
Preparing to Write an Essay

📖 **Chapter 1:** Tools for Good Writing

Have you ever watched workers building a house? You might have noticed that electricians, plumbers, carpenters, and other workers use a variety of tools to help them do the job. Every worker knows that the better the tools are, the better the work will be. Like builders constructing a house, you will need a good set of tools to write well. This unit will help to supply you with some of the necessary tools and knowledge to do your best on the **Grade 6 PSSA Writing Assessment.**

CHAPTER 1

TOOLS FOR GOOD WRITING

It helps to have a good set of tools to become a better writer. This chapter will introduce you to some of the tools you will need to write well. Before we look at what it takes to be a good writer, let's see what you think is needed to write well.

THINK ABOUT IT

What do you think makes someone a good writer?

When you wrote your answer, you may have noticed that you followed two steps:

★ First, you had to think about what you wanted to say.

★ Second, you had to be able to express your thoughts in words.

6

Good writers write clearly so that readers understand the thoughts they are expressing. A reader should be able to picture in his or her mind the same thoughts the writer was trying to express when he or she wrote.

A good writer is able to write down thoughts in a way that the reader can picture the same thoughts.

THE BASIC TOOLS OF WRITING

There are **three basic tools** for writing: *words, sentences,* and *paragraphs.* Just as carpenters have rules about how to use their tools, there are also some basic rules about the proper use of words, sentences, and paragraphs. In this chapter, we will review these basic rules.

WORDS

PARTS OF SPEECH

There are many kinds of words. We sometimes label a word as a **part of speech.** This has to do with the role the word plays in a sentence.

★ **Nouns.** A noun is a word that names a person, place, or thing. Examples of nouns are: *man, house, town,* and *apple.*

★ **Pronouns.** A pronoun is a word that takes the place of a noun used earlier in the writing. Examples of pronouns are: *I, we, you, he, she, her, him, they,* and *it.*

★ **Verbs.** Verbs tell what a person or thing is doing or feeling or what is being done to it. Many verbs are action words that describe some kind of action. Examples of verbs are: *jump, walk, run, dance, eat, think, feel, have* and *is.*

★ **Adjectives.** An adjective describes a noun. Adjectives add color and mood to a sentence. Examples of adjectives are: *red, rich, soft, beautiful, sad,* and *kind.*

★ **Adverbs.** Adverbs tell about verbs, adjectives, or even other adverbs. They are used by writers to tell *where, when,* and *how* an action happens. Examples of adverbs are: *often, quickly, never, always, very,* and *slowly.*

★ **Prepositions.** A preposition tells about the position of a noun or pronoun. It links the noun or pronoun to something in the rest of the sentence. Examples of prepositions are: *with, over, above, below,* and *of.*

CHECKING YOUR UNDERSTANDING

Identify the part of speech of the following words:

quickly _____   slept _____

lemon _____   him _____

is _____   under _____

crunchy _____   green _____

CHOOSING THE BEST WORD

When you write, you should choose the most exact words that you can. This makes it easier for your reader to make a mental picture of what you are writing about. Words that help the reader to see, hear, taste, smell, or feel what you are writing about make it easier for the reader to picture your thoughts and make your writing more interesting. Your choice of words helps make up your **style.**

CHECKING YOUR UNDERSTANDING

Check (✔) the word in each pair of words that is more exact:

❑ store　　　　　　**or**　　　　❑ McGill's Department Store

❑ convertible　　　　**or**　　　　❑ car

❑ vegetable　　　　　**or**　　　　❑ carrots

STYLE

Check (✔) the word or phrase that you think would better help a reader picture what the writer is trying to say:

❑ lion　　　　　　　**or**　　　　❑ animal

❑ bird　　　　　　　**or**　　　　❑ blue jay

Let's see if you can make your own writing more descriptive. Take the word given on the left. Add details to it so that the reader can *see, hear, taste,* or *feel* the word. The first example has been done for you.

★ apple: _____ *a cold, green apple* _____

★ car: _____

★ table: _____

★ shirt: _____

★ pencil: _____

SENTENCES

WHAT IS A SENTENCE?

A sentence is a group of words that expresses a complete thought. The first word in a sentence is always capitalized. Every sentence must end with a *period, question mark,* or *exclamation point.* Each sentence always has a subject and a predicate.

★ The **subject** is *who* or *what* the sentence is about. The subject is a noun or pronoun.

★ The **predicate** is what the subject *does* or *what happens to the subject* in the sentence. It provides the action of the sentence. The predicate uses a verb.

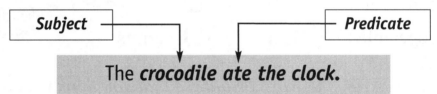

| Subject | | Predicate |

The **crocodile ate the clock.**

CHECKING YOUR UNDERSTANDING

Write three sentences.
(Circle) *the subject and* <u>underline</u> *the predicate.*

1. _____

   _____

2. _____

   _____

3. _____

   _____

Together, the subject and predicate of a sentence should express a complete thought. If you read a sentence by itself, it should make sense to you. Do not be fooled by a group of words that look like a sentence. If they do not express a complete thought, they do not make up a sentence.

CHECKING YOUR UNDERSTANDING

Check (✔) the examples that are complete sentences.

❑ Before I went to school.

❑ They watched television.

❑ He ate fish yesterday.

❑ Because she was thirsty.

Now let's use what you have learned to write some interesting and descriptive sentences. Take the basic sentence you find in the first column and add color or some other description to it by using adjectives and adverbs. Then tell when or where the action in the sentence took place. The first sentence has been done for you.

Prepositional Phrase

Basic Sentence	Add Description	Tell When & Where
The man walked.	The man in the yellow sweater walked quietly. Adverb Adjective	On a rainy night, the man in the yellow sweater walked quietly past the gas station. STYLE
The boy ate.		
The tree fell down.		
The woman read the newspaper.		

PARAGRAPHS

A **paragraph** is a group of sentences that deals with the same subject or topic. Each new paragraph is generally **indented,** except in letters or some printed texts. Often, a paragraph has a **topic sentence** that identifies the subject of the paragraph. The rest of the paragraph has details that tell about the subject identified by the topic sentence.

CHECKING YOUR UNDERSTANDING

> Erica enjoys her job as an elementary school teacher. She loves watching her students' faces when they learn something for the first time. She also likes learning more about the different subjects she has to teach. Most of all, she feels that she is making a contribution to the world by helping the young people in her classroom to become responsible citizens.

★ Underline the topic sentence of this paragraph.   `FOCUS`

★ If you were writing this paragraph and wanted to add some more details about Erica, what might you write?   `CONTENT`

_____

_____

_____

There is no general rule about how long a paragraph should be. However, if your paragraph is very long, it can probably be broken down into two or more paragraphs. See if information in the paragraph can be divided up, based on different aspects of the topic.

If you decide to divide your writing into more than one paragraph, be sure to let your reader know you are starting a new paragraph by going to the next line and indenting.

UNIT 2:
THE CHARACTERISTICS OF GOOD WRITING:
THE FIVE SCOREABLE DOMAINS

📖 **Chapter 2:** Focus and Content

📖 **Chapter 3:** Organization and Style

📖 **Chapter 4:** Writing Conventions

In this unit you will learn about the five characteristics or domains of good writing that your essay should have — focus, content, organization, style, and writing conventions. In Chapter 2 you will learn about the domains of focus and content. Chapter 3 looks at the domains of organization and style. Chapter 4 briefly explores the domain of writing conventions.

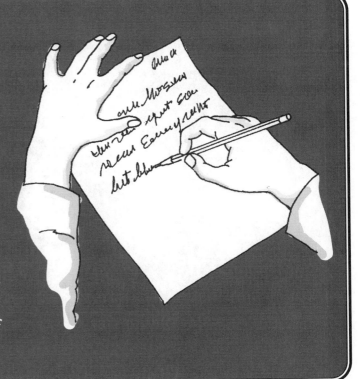

CHAPTER 2

FOCUS AND CONTENT

When you read, you try to understand the writer's ideas. When you write, you try to communicate your own ideas to the reader.

In order to communicate well, your writing should have five important characteristics. Each of these characteristics of good writing make up a **domain.** These five domains are the elements of good writing:

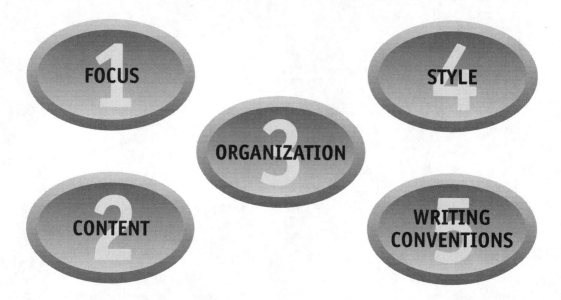

On the **Grade 6 PSSA Writing Assessment,** each of the five domains of good writing — *focus, content, organization, style,* and *writing conventions* — is scored separately on a 4-point scale. A score of **3** or **4** represents writing that is either acceptable or excellent for that domain. However, a score of **0, 1,** or **2** in a domain is considered to be unacceptable writing. This unit will explain each of the domains of good writing.

THE WRITING PROMPT

On the writing test, you will be given a writing prompt. A **prompt** is a statement that encourages you to think. It causes you to respond in some way. The **Grade 6 PSSA Writing Assessment** will have two sessions. Each session will require you to respond to *one* writing prompt.

Both writing prompts on the **Grade 6 PSSA Writing Assessment** will consist of several parts. Let's examine each of these parts:

DIRECTIONS

The directions will tell you how much time you have to plan, write, and proofread your response.

PLANNING AND WRITING REMINDERS

The planning and writing reminders will keep you focused on the characteristics your writing should contain. They provide hints on how to go about planning and writing your essay.

THE INTRODUCTORY STATEMENT

The introductory statement will provide background to the writing assignment. This statement will introduce a situation you will have to write about.

THE TASK STATEMENT

The statement identifies the type of writing you are required to create — a *narrative, informative,* or *persuasive* essay — and the question on which your writing must be focused.

THE GUIDELINES

The guidelines will identify specific requirements that your writing assignment should meet. Each guideline corresponds to one of the "scoreable domains" —*focus, content, organization, style,* and ***writing conventions.***

The following page contains a sample prompt similar to one you might find on the writing test. Let's look at this sample prompt and each of its specific parts.

You will have one class period (but no more than 60 minutes if your class is longer) to plan, write, and proofread your response, making any necessary corrections.

Directions

Planning

- Think about what you want to write.
- Reread the prompt to make sure you are writing about the topic.
- Make notes. Use your prewriting skills, such as mapping or outlining.
- Carefully read the five statements below the prompt. Each statement refers to one of the scoreable domains: focus, content, organization, style, and conventions.

Writing

- Write your essay on the paper your teacher gives you.
- Proofread your essay and make necessary corrections.

Planning and Writing Reminders

READ THE ENTIRE PROMPT CAREFULLY.

Introductory Statement

Sixth grade can provide many special memories.

Write about one person that you would like to remember from sixth grade.

Task Statement

As you write your paper remember to:

- Tell who that person is and why you want to remember him or her.
- Use specific details to develop your narrative.
- Present your ideas in a clear and logical order, including an introduction, body, and conclusion.
- Use a variety of words and well-constructed sentences.
- Correct any errors in grammar, mechanics, spelling, usage, and sentence formation.

Guidelines

Now you know what the prompt on the writing test will look like. Let's begin to look more closely at the five domains of good writing. The rest of this chapter will examine **focus** and **content**.

FOCUS

> **Focus:** "The single controlling point made with an awareness of task (mode) about a specific topic."
>
> **Score of 4:** Sharp, distinct controlling point made about a single topic with evident awareness of task (mode)

Focus means your writing should stay on the task you are expected to write about. Choose a specific topic based on the writing prompt. Stick to that topic! Everything in your essay should be focused on answering the task. Avoid including information not related to your topic.

Usually, you will be making some single controlling point about a topic in response to the task. For example, you might respond to the prompt on page 16 by writing about an interesting person you met in sixth grade. You would focus on one characteristic or event that made the person memorable. Everything in your essay should relate to the person.

CHECKING YOUR UNDERSTANDING

*Suppose you were writing about your classroom pet.
Place a check mark (✔) next to all sentences that would be
within the focus of your writing.*

❑ Our classroom pet is Mr. Whiskers, a white rabbit.

❑ This Thursday, we will be seeing a movie in class.

❑ Mr. Whiskers eats lettuce, carrots, and other vegetables.

❑ Mr. Whiskers lives in a cage at the back of our classroom.

❑ Each day we clean the cage and give Mr. Whiskers fresh water.

❑ Gerbils make good classroom pets.

FOCUS

CONTENT

> **Content:** "The presence of ideas developed through facts, examples, anecdotes, details, opinions, statistics, reasons, and/or explanations."
>
> **Score of 4:** Substantial, specific, and/or illustrative content demonstrating strong development and sophisticated explanation.

Content refers to the ideas, details, and examples you use to support or explain the topic you write about in response to the prompt. When you write, *your job* is to provide the supporting details that explain your ideas.

WHEN YOU NARRATE

If you are telling about an experience, describe each event in detail. Tell about the *who, what, when, where, how,* and *why* of each event. Be as specific as you can.

CHECKING YOUR UNDERSTANDING

Describe the most important things you did this morning before you left your house for school: CONTENT

1. _____

2. _____

3. _____

WHEN YOU WRITE TO INFORM

If you are writing to inform, give specific ideas, facts, details, and examples to support each part of your explanation. Put yourself in your reader's shoes. Think about what your reader needs to know to understand what you are explaining. Be sure to include those details in order.

CHECKING YOUR UNDERSTANDING

Provide details about your favorite activity or pastime:

What is it? _____

When do you do it? _____

Where do you do it? _____

How do you do it? _____

Why do you do it? _____

CONTENT

WHEN YOU WRITE TO PERSUADE

When you take a position on an issue, give reasons for taking that position. For each reason, list or describe specific ideas, details, and examples that explain or support your position.

CHECKING YOUR UNDERSTANDING

CONTENT

Are you a neat or messy person?
Decide which position you would take in the following controversy and list two reasons to support your position:

Reasons why a messy room is acceptable:	*Reasons why a messy room should not be acceptable:*
1. _____ _____	1. _____ _____
2. _____ _____	2. _____ _____

CHAPTER 3

ORGANIZATION AND STYLE

ORGANIZATION

Organization: "The order developed and sustained within and across paragraphs using transitional devices and including introduction and conclusion."

Score of 4: Sophisticated arrangement of content with evident and/or subtle transitions.

Organization, the third element of good writing refers to how you put your ideas together. Imagine someone who built a house with the roof at the bottom and the basement on top. The house would soon collapse!

In the same way, your response on the **PSSA Writing Assessment** has to be put together in a *logical* and *orderly way.* If your organization is not logical, your reader will not be able to follow what you are writing about. Your answer should be organized into three main parts: *introduction*, *body*, and *conclusion.* Let's look at each of these parts more closely.

 ## THE INTRODUCTION

When we first meet someone, we introduce ourselves. Similarly, your essay should begin with an introduction where you tell your reader what you are writing about.

It is in the introduction that you focus on presenting your main idea or position taken in response to the directions of the prompt. From your introduction, your reader will know at the start what to expect in the rest of your essay.

THE BODY

The body is the main part of your essay answer. Here is where you focus on giving details and examples to support the assertions or position taken in the introduction. Be as descriptive as possible. Use all five senses in describing things. Include plenty of details and examples to help your reader understand your ideas.

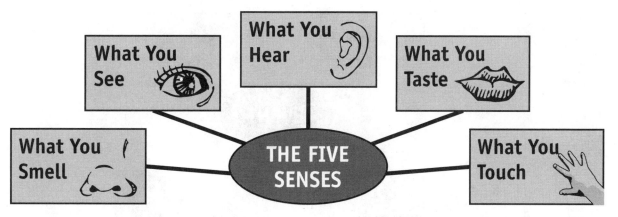

Within the body of your essay, be sure to organize your ideas and details in some logical order. This makes it easy for the reader to follow your ideas. How you organize your writing will depend on what you are writing about. There are four main ways that good writers use to put their writing in logical order:

★ **Time Order.** If you are telling about an event or experience, the first paragraph should include an umbrella statement identifying the entire experience you are going to write about. Then tell about things in more detail in the order in which they happened.

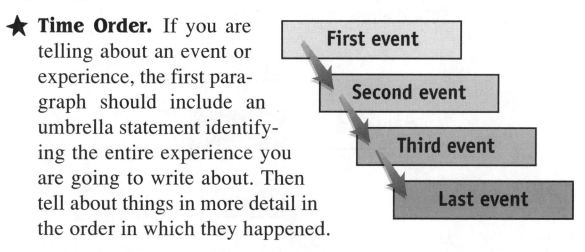

Start by telling about the first event. Describe the event by telling about the *who, what, when, where, how,* and *why.* Then move on to the second event. Proceed in time order until you completely describe all the events that made up the experience.

★ **Cause-and-Effect Order.** If you are explaining the causes and effects of an important event, one way is to begin by describing all of the causes. After you have described the causes of the event, then describe the event's effects. Another way to write about causes and effects is to describe each cause and its particular effects, one at a time.

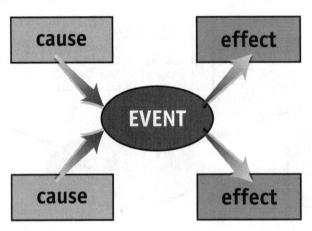

★ **Space Order.** If you are describing an object or scene in your writing, imagine the object or scene in your mind. Then pick some point and begin to describe it. Move left to right, or up and down as you continue your description. Be sure to continue in the same direction for the rest of the description.

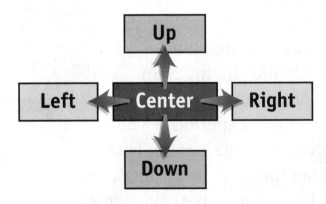

★ **Order of Importance.** If you have a main idea and a number of examples or supporting details, give the general or main idea first. Then provide the supporting details in order of their importance. Give the most important example or reason first. You can also start with the least important first and move to the most important.

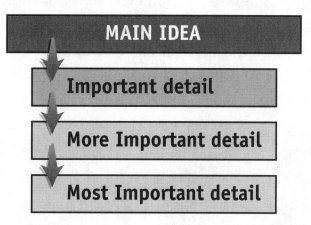

CHECKING YOUR UNDERSTANDING

Number each of the following sentences in the order you would place them in a logically organized paragraph.

☐ To the right, he could see British troops pulling their cannons.

☐ Justin looked in amazement at the scene in front of him.

☐ To the left he could see the red uniforms of the British troops.

☐ In the center of the field, he could see hundreds of British cavalry.

ORGANIZATION

☐ Justin realized he needed to contact General Washington at once.

CONCLUSION

When we leave someone, we normally say goodbye. At the end of your essay, you should similarly say goodbye to your reader by writing a conclusion. The conclusion signals to the reader that the writing is coming to an end. There are many ways to conclude your writing. You may want to briefly summarize the main ideas of the body of your writing. You may also want to state some general moral or lesson that can be learned from what you have written.

A NOTE ABOUT TRANSITION WORDS

An important part of organizing your writing is to use <u>transition words</u>. Transition words act as signposts. These words tell a reader you are moving from one point to another. When readers see these signposts, they know they are moving in the right direction. Some useful transition words and phrases include:

★ When giving a list of points, use number words like <u>first</u>, <u>second</u>, and <u>third</u>. Each time the reader sees a new number, he or she will know that you have moved to a new idea or new point.

★ When telling about events, you can often use the day of the week or time of year as a transition. Other useful transitions include <u>the next day</u>, <u>the following week</u>, <u>later that year</u>, and <u>next</u>.

★ Other common transition words include: <u>for example</u>, <u>therefore</u>, <u>also</u>, <u>in addition</u>, <u>another</u>, and <u>then</u>.

CHECKING YOUR UNDERSTANDING

In the following paragraph (circle) *each word or phrase that is used as a transition:*   `ORGANIZATION`

On Tuesday, Robin went to the market. Later that evening, she bought some steaks at the supermarket. The following day, Robin invited some of her friends over to her backyard. After sitting around and talking, they barbecued the steaks. By midnight, her friends finally left to go home. Exhausted from the day's activities, Robin fell fast asleep on her couch.

THE USE OF PRONOUNS TO HOLD YOUR ESSAY TOGETHER

Pronouns — such as *he, she, they,* and *their* — help "glue" your essay together by connecting sentences. If you use a noun, you can refer to it with a pronoun in later sentences. This helps to tie your writing together for the reader.

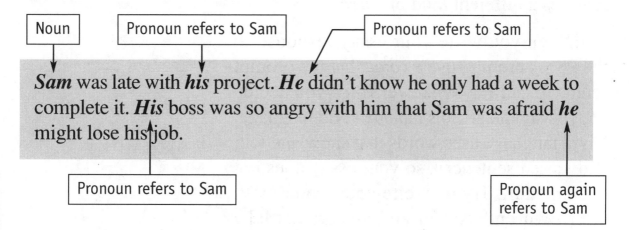

| Noun | Pronoun refers to Sam | | Pronoun refers to Sam |

Sam was late with *his* project. *He* didn't know he only had a week to complete it. *His* boss was so angry with him that Sam was afraid *he* might lose his job.

| Pronoun refers to Sam | | Pronoun again refers to Sam |

STYLE

> **Style:** "The choice, use and arrangement of words and sentence structures that create tone and voice."
>
> **Score of 4:** Precise, illustrative use of a variety of words and sentence structures to create consistent writer's voice and tone appropriate to audience.

You know that not everyone wears the same type of clothing. People wear different styles to express themselves. There are different styles in writing, too. Just as with clothing, the style that you use to write can express what you think and how you feel.

Your choice of style is what is called **voice** in writing. You create *voice* by the words and sentence structures you use. Your writing can be funny or formal, serious or scary. Each of these forms of writing requires a different kind of *voice*.

When you write your essay response to the PSSA prompt, use a *voice* that the prompt seems to call for. Whatever *voice* you decide on, you should always include vivid language. Vivid language uses words that show and tell, and varied sentences, so your essay does not become dull. Try to excite your reader with your own enthusiasm and sincerity. Make there hear that *voice*.

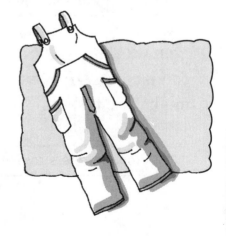

Also remember that it would be quite boring if you used the same tone when you write. You naturally vary the **tone** and volume of your voice as you talk about an event that is exciting or interesting. Your writing needs that same kind of variety and excitement

The *tone* of your writing reflects your feelings and attitudes towards what you are writing about. Always keep your writing *tone* in tune with the subject you are writing about and the audience you are writing for. For example, a comic tone would not be appropriate if you are writing an informational essay or narrating a tragic event.

CHAPTER 4

WRITING CONVENTIONS

In addition to having a clear focus, specific ideas, a logical organization, and an interesting style, you must express yourself correctly when you write. Otherwise, readers will have a hard time understanding what it is that you have to say.

WHY WE HAVE WRITING CONVENTIONS

Conventions: "Grammar, mechanics, spelling, usage and sentence formation."

Score of 4: Evident control of grammar, mechanics, spelling, usage, and sentence formation.

The fifth characteristic of good writing is following accepted **writing conventions.** Over the years, certain conventions have developed for what is accepted as standard in spelling, grammar, capitalization, and punctuation. These conventions provide rules for how we should express ourselves. By following these rules, we can understand each other more easily.

In this chapter, you will learn some of the most important conventions for standard written English. You will receive a score from 1 to 4 on the **PSSA Writing Assessment** based on how well you follow the conventions of standard written English.

Writers most often make mistakes in the following areas:

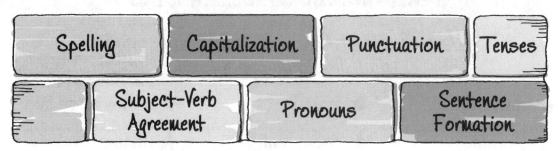

SPELLING

Hundreds of years ago there were no rules for spelling in English. People spelled each word in their own way. Today, we have rules for spelling words. Most words can be spelled in only one way.

Because the English language has been influenced by other languages, certain *sounds* are not always spelled the same way. This makes it harder to know how to spell some words. When you misspell a word or learn a new word, you should look carefully at the word. Often there is a "hot spot" that makes the word difficult to spell. Focus on the "hot spot." Make a circle around it. Then write the word several times from memory. Keep a list of words you have difficulty spelling. Practice spelling them.

CHECKING YOUR UNDERSTANDING

Circle the "hot spot" in each of the following words.

Tuesday	receive	weather	balloon	Wednesday
across	there	coming	pleasant	address
their	February	friend	afraid	separate

CONVENTIONS

CAPITALIZATION

You should always start each sentence with a capital letter. In addition, all proper nouns are capitalized. A **proper noun** is the name of a specific person, place, or thing. For example, *Michael Jordan, Philadelphia,* and the *Declaration of Independence* are all proper nouns.

CHECKING YOUR UNDERSTANDING

Underline each letter of the following nouns that should be capitalized.

CONVENTIONS

★ mr. smith   ★ bread   ★ strawberry jam

★ florida   ★ meat loaf   ★ disneyland

PUNCTUATION

Here are some of the main rules for the correct use of punctuation:

★ Use commas to separate items in a list, dates, and quotations. Also use commas to separate a city from its state or country, or to separate some opening clauses from the rest of the sentence.

> Lenny brought tomatoes, eggs, milk, and a loaf of bread, to his hotel room in Paris, France.

★ Use periods at the end of abbreviations.

> Mr., Ms., Mrs., U.S.A.

★ Use apostrophes to show possession or contractions.

> Jack's boat   I'm = I am

★ Use quotation marks for direct speech.

> "I want to go home," she said loudly.

SENTENCE ENDINGS

You should always end a sentence with a *period, question mark,* or *exclamation point.* The punctuation you use will depend on the type of sentence you have written.

★ End each statement with a period.

> The hungry monkeys ate a bunch of bananas**.**

★ End each question with a question mark.

> What time is it**?**

★ End sentences that show strong feelings, such as surprise, laughter or some other strong emotion, with an exclamation point.

> You look absolutely ridiculous with that hat on your head**!**

CHECKING YOUR UNDERSTANDING

Add the final punctuation to each of these sentences.

★ The baker took the hot loaves of bread from the oven ☐

★ Where is the best place to buy a computer ☐

★ I have never been happier in all my life ☐   CONVENTIONS

Insert the correct punctuation in the following paragraph:

It was late at night on October 13 ☐ 1995 ☐ Everything was quiet in the house ☐ Suddenly we heard a crash ☐ A large number of people rushed out of their homes to see what was going on ☐ ☐ Is anyone hurt ☐ ☐ our neighbor asked ☐ ☐ It looks as if there was an earthquake ☐ ☐ my mother answered ☐

SUBJECT-VERB AGREEMENT

The subject and verb of a sentence should always "agree" with each other.

★ If the subject of a sentence is singular, you should use a verb in the singular form.

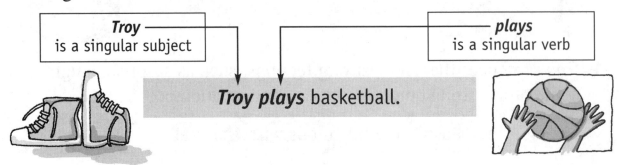

| **Troy**
is a singular subject | | **plays**
is a singular verb |

Troy plays basketball.

★ If the subject of a sentence is plural, you should use a verb in the plural form.

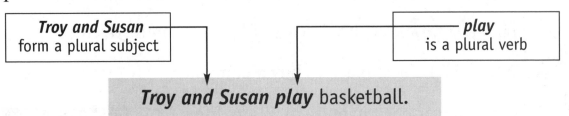

| **Troy and Susan**
form a plural subject | | **play**
is a plural verb |

Troy and Susan play basketball.

CHECKING YOUR UNDERSTANDING

See if you can choose the correct verb in each of the following:

1. They (*are eating* / *is eating*) lunch.

2. They (*have* / *has*) many pets in their home.

3. He (*wakes* / *wake*) up each morning at 7:00 o'clock.

4. Susan's grandmother (*live* / *lives*) in Chicago, Illinois.

5. Joan (*walk* / *walks*) to school each morning.

CONVENTIONS

PRONOUN FORMS

Pronouns take the place of nouns. Pronouns take different forms when they are used to do different jobs in a sentence.

★ If the pronoun is the subject, use *I, you, he, she, it, we,* or *they.*

> **He** is going to karate class.

★ If the pronoun is not the subject of the sentence, use *me, you, him, her, it, us,* and *them.*

> Chinami gave **them** the present.
> Carson sent a birthday card to **her**.

CHECKING YOUR UNDERSTANDING

Select the correct pronoun to complete the following sentences:

1. Judy and (**I** / **me**) went to the zoo for a visit.

2. (**She** / **Her**) baked (**he** / **him**) a cake for his birthday.

3. (**They** / **Them**) like to go bowling on Saturday.

Some pronouns raise special problems. Here are three groups that often cause confusion:

★ **It's / Its**

It's is a contraction for two words — *it* and *is*:

> **It's** time to go to bed.

Its without an apostrophe shows possession:

> The stray cat was missing **its** owner.

★ There / their / they're

There means a place:

> He lives over *there*.

Their shows possession:

> *Their* car is waiting.

They're is a contraction for two words — *they are*:

> *They're* going away.

★ Your / You're

Your shows possession:

> Is this *your* boat?

You're means *you are*:

> *You're* in a good mood today.

CHECKING YOUR UNDERSTANDING

Select the correct form of the word to complete the following sentences:

1. (*Its / It's*) time for us to go home.

2. Are these (*your / you're*) hat and gloves?

3. (*There / Their / They're*) is where the monster lives.

4. It seems that (*your / you're*) in my chair.

CONVENTIONS

VERB TENSES

Verbs take different forms, known as **tenses,** to tell us when an action takes place. Different tenses are used to express actions in the *past, present,* and *future.*

Past Tense	Present Tense	Future Tense
He liked her.	He likes her.	He will like her.
She was eating.	She is eating.	She will be eating.

Be sure to keep your verbs in the right tense. If a story takes place in the past, keep all the verbs in the past tense. Change the tense of the verb only if the action moves to the present or future.

Last week, the grumpy sailor *ate* at the old inn. He *had* a meal of fish and *washed* it down with some wine. Then he *went* to sleep in the loft in the stables above the horses. Next week, he *will go* back to work with the new captain of the ship.

Notice how the first three sentences are all happening in the past. In the last sentence, the action switches to something that will take place in the future. As a result, the verb changes to the future tense.

SENTENCE FORMATION

When writing, avoid *sentence fragments* and *run-on sentences.*

SENTENCE FRAGMENTS

A sentence fragment does not express a complete thought. One common error is to begin a clause with a *subordinate conjunction,* such as **when, since, as, because, although,** and not connect it to another clause to make a complete sentence. A clause beginning with a subordinate conjunction is never a complete sentence: *Because he wants it.* It should be connected to an independent clause: *Because he wants it, he is willing to work for it.*

RUN-ON SENTENCES

Separate sentences cannot be joined together by commas. This creates a run-on sentence. Break a run-on sentence into two sentences, or use conjunctions to join the separate clauses together. Use **and, or, but,** or subordinate conjunctions like **when, since, as, because,** and **although.**

COMBINING SENTENCES

It would be quite boring if every sentence was the same. Use different kinds of sentences to keep your writing interesting. You can combine sentences by using words such as **and** and **but.** You can also use special words like **since, because, who, while,** and **although** to combine sentences. Let's look at some examples:

Two Sentences

Peter likes to eat nuts.	Mary enjoys eating fruit.

One Sentence

Peter likes to eat nuts, **but** Mary enjoys eating fruit.

Two Sentences

Al went shopping in the store.
His sister Mary went to the library.

One Sentence

Al went shopping in the store, **while** his sister Mary
went to the library.

CHECKING YOUR UNDERSTANDING

Combine the following pairs of sentences.
Use the word in parentheses to join them.

(Who)   Michael Jordan is a famous basketball player. He played for the Chicago Bulls.

(But)   I enjoy playing baseball. I do not like to play basketball.

CONVENTIONS

CHECKING YOUR WRITING FOR ERRORS

A ship's lookout is constantly checking to be sure that nothing gets in the way of the ship's safety. When you write, you should play the role of a ship's lookout. You must always be on the lookout for writing errors. Keep reviewing what you are writing. This will help you catch writing errors that could distract and confuse your readers.

Practice Exercises

Directions: Answer the following questions dealing with writing conventions.

1. **Which of the following is written correctly?**
   A Americans declared their independence on July 4, 1776.
   B Americans declared their independence on july 4, 1776.
   C Americans declared their independence on July 4. 1776.
   D Americans declared their Independence on july 4. 1776.

2. **Which of the following is a complete sentence?**
   A Because he wanted to sleep.   C Not now.
   B She ate a candy bar.   D At three o'clock.

3. **Which of these sentences in the paragraph below is NOT a complete sentence?**

   (1) Ben wanted to go home. (2) His mother wanted to stay. (3) At least until lunch. (4) Then she wanted to go, too.

   A Sentence 1   C Sentence 3
   B Sentence 2   D Sentence 4

4. *Deirdre missed the bus. She arrived late to school.*

 Which is the best way to combine these sentences without changing their meaning?

 A Deirdre missed the bus, and arrived late to school.

 B Deirdre missed the bus, but she arrived late to school.

 C Because Deirdre missed the bus, she arrived late to school.

 D Deirdre missed the bus, since she arrived late to school.

5. *He'll eat dinner. He'll go to sleep.*

 Which is the best way to combine these sentences without changing their meaning?

 A He'll eat dinner, and then go to sleep.

 B He'll eat dinner and go to sleep.

 C He'll eat dinner, and he'll go to sleep.

 D He'll eat dinner, or he'll go to sleep.

Directions: Replace the underlined part of each sentence with the best of the four choices.

6. **This time of year is my <u>favorite, all</u> the birds are singing.**

 A favorite. All

 B favorite, all

 C favorite? All

 D favorite, All

7. **They <u>was getting they're</u> things ready for the trip.**

 A was getting they're

 B were getting they're

 C were getting their

 D was getting there

The following letter has several mistakes.

> Dear Julie,
>
> Today was very important day? I bought my first pet. His name is piggles. He is a guinea pig. piggles eats lettuce hay and special pellets for guinea pigs. He live in a cage. Most of the day he sleeps, at night he runs around the cage. I plays with him every morning before and after school.
>
> Your friend,
> Taylor

Use the lines below to rewrite the letter without mistakes.

Dear Julie,

_____

_____

_____

_____

_____

_____

_____

_____

_____

Your friend,

_____

UNIT 3: TYPES OF ESSAYS

📖 **Chapter 5:** Responding to a Writing Prompt

📖 **Chapter 6:** Writing a Narrative Essay

📖 **Chapter 7:** Writing an Informational Essay

📖 **Chapter 8:** Writing a Persuasive Essay

The **Grade 6 PSSA Writing Assessment** currently consists of two writing prompts. You must respond to both prompts. You will have 60 minutes to respond to each of these writing prompts. You must be prepared to write at least two out of a possible three types of essays — either a narrative, informational, or persuasive essay. In this unit you will learn how to respond to a writing prompt by answering each of the three types of essays you may face.

CHAPTER 5

RESPONDING TO A WRITING PROMPT

In the last chapter you learned about the basic elements of good writing. Now let's turn our attention to how you should respond to a writing prompt to produce your best answer.

There are four main steps in responding to the writing prompt on the **Grade 6 PSSA Writing Assessment:**

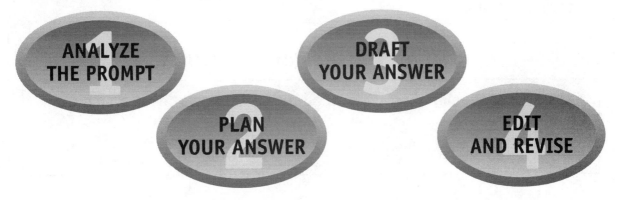

STEP 1: ANALYZE THE PROMPT

As you know, the **PSSA Writing Test** will present you with a writing prompt.

The **first part** of the writing prompt will describe a situation or provide background to the writing assignment.

The **second part** of the writing prompt will have specific directions on what you should write about. This assignment provides a focus for your writing.

Let's look at a sample prompt:

You will have one class period (but no more than 60 minutes if your class is longer) to plan, write, and proofread your response, making any necessary corrections.

Planning

- Think about what you want to write.
- Reread the prompt to make sure you are writing about the topic.
- Make notes. Use your prewriting skills, such as mapping or outlining.
- Carefully read the five statements below the prompt. Each statement refers to one of the scoreable domains: focus, content, organization, style, and conventions.

Writing

- Write your essay on the paper your teacher gives you.
- Proofread your essay and make necessary corrections.

READ THE ENTIRE PROMPT CAREFULLY.

> **Your family is deciding whether to go to the movies or have a picnic this weekend.**
>
> **Write to persuade your family to support your choice.**

As you write your paper remember to:

- Clearly state whether your family should go the movies or have a picnic.

- Include specific facts, details, reasons, and examples to persuade your family to support your choice.

- Present your ideas in a clear and logical order, including an introduction, body, and conclusion.

- Use a variety of words and well-constructed sentences.

- Correct any errors in grammar, mechanics, spelling, usage, and sentence formation.

To analyze this prompt, you should take the following steps:

★ First, you must determine the type of writing you are being asked to create. In the sample prompt, are you asked to give information, write a persuasive essay, or describe a personal experience?

> *The prompt asks you to write a persuasive essay. It clearly states in the writing prompt, "write to persuade."*

★ Examine any question words or commands in the directions and the guidelines of the prompt. The first guideline will usually echo the directions and state the focus of your writing. For example, do the directions ask you to write about, describe, persuade, explain how or explain why?

> *In the sample prompt, you have to persuade your family to agree with your position — whether to go to the movies or to have a picnic.*

★ Now take a moment to think about the task in the writing prompt. Use the hints or clues provided in the directions and guidelines to spur your thinking.

> *In this sample prompt, your task is to tell whether your family should go to the movies or have a picnic. Think about which you would rather do and the reasons behind your choice.*

or

STEP 2: PLAN YOUR ANSWER

 The next step in the writing process is to *plan* your answer. For many students, this the hardest part of responding to a writing prompt. You need to think of what you want to write about. One way to get ideas is to jot down notes on different items you might write about. Then look them over to see which best responds to the directions in the prompt. You will learn more about this technique in later chapters.

After you select your main idea or have made a choice, start to fill in the details. It sometimes helps to create an **outline** or **topic map** to organize your thoughts about the task in the prompt.

★ **Outlining.** An outline is used by writers to help break down large ideas, events, or concepts into smaller units. Writers generally use Roman (I, II, III) and Arabic (1, 2, 3) numerals as well as capital (A, B, C) and small (a, b, c) letters to make an outline.

Let's see what an outline might look like if you were asked to write in response to the prompt on page 42.

> REASONS FOR A PICNIC
> I.   Picnics Provide Exercise
>   A. Walking to the picnic grounds
>   B. Playing outdoor games
> II.   Picnics Provide Opportunity to Talk
> III.   Picnics Are A Lot of Fun
>   A. Family will never agree on same movie
>   1. Movies are too much like T.V.
>   2. Can't talk to each other
>   B. Family can mingle while eating

★ **Clustering or Mapping.** Another pre-writing format is clustering or mapping. To make your plan in the form of a concept map or cluster, put your main idea or topic in the middle of the paper. Then surround this idea or topic with supporting facts, details, and examples. You can surround these details, in turn, with further descriptive information. Again, responding to the same sample prompt:

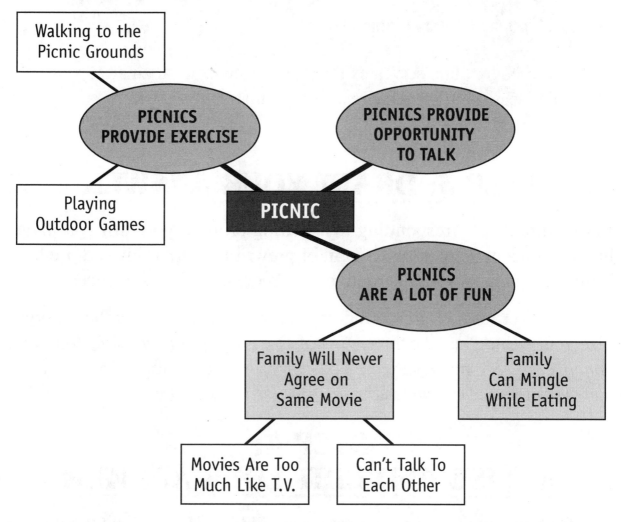

Another pre-writing method is to outline your answer in the form of a hamburger.

★ The **top bun** serves as your *introduction.*

★ The **patties of meat** form the *body of your answer.*

★ The **bottom bun** is your *conclusion.*

The top bun serves as the place
where you identify the event you are describing,
your main idea, or the position you are taking
in response to the prompt.

The patties of meat make up the body of your essay. Here you list reasons, specific details, and examples to support the main idea you stated in the introduction.

The bottom bun serves as the place where you summarize your main ideas and remind the reader of your strongest points.

STEP 3: DRAFT YOUR ANSWER

In the third step of responding to a writing prompt, you turn your hamburger, concept map, or other form of prewriting into a finished product. Turn each point of your plan into one or more complete sentences.

Whatever form of prewriting or planning you use, remember to organize your writing into the three parts of an essay — *introduction, body,* and *conclusion.* Also make sure the body of your essay is logically organized and stays focused on the task or writing assignment.

STEP 4: REVISE AND EDIT YOUR ANSWER

The first person to read your writing should be **YOU** — *not* the person who is scoring your writing. Always read over your work before you hand it in.

Read your written draft silently to yourself. Pretend you are someone else, reading it for the very first time. Make sure that you have included all your major ideas.

As you review what you have written, ask yourself some questions. If your answer is "no" to any of the following questions, your response is not finished and needs further work:

★ Have you written the *type of essay* — *narrative, informative,* or *persuasive* — required by the writing prompt?

★ Did you *follow the directions and guidelines* of the writing prompt?

★ Does your writing have a *focus*?

★ Have you *stayed on the topic*?

★ Do you have an *introduction, body,* and *conclusion*?

★ Does the body of your essay have a *logical organization*?

★ Have you *provided details, examples,* and *reasons* to support or explain your position or main idea?

★ Is the *style* — tone and voice — of your essay in keeping with what you have to say?

★ *Could a person reading your paper for the first time understand what you mean?*

Here is where you have the opportunity to "fine-tune" what you have written. Revise your draft by rewriting any sections that are poorly organized. Add ideas and details you may have left out. Take out any extra information that does not relate to the topic or theme of your writing.

On the **Grade 6 PSSA Writing Assessment,** you can just cross out any words or sections you want to take out, and you can add words or sentences using arrows. Also edit your writing by checking for errors in writing conventions. Watch out for mistakes in spelling, grammar, punctuation, and usage. Use some of the proofreading marks below to help you edit.

COMMON PROOFREADING MARKS

ℓ	= cross out a word, phrase, or sentence
c̲	= capitalize the letter
¶	= start a new paragraph
ⱷ	= make a capital letter lower case
⊙	= insert a period
∧	= insert a word or phrase

Here is what a revised paragraph might look like after you have made corrections.

One of the ∧**most** exciting and interesting things that ∧**ever** happened to me was going to ro̲me with my mother. When I was nine ∧**years old,** my mother decided to take me along. My mother was ~~in charge~~ ∧**the manager** of the dress department at a large ∧**downtown** department store. Every ⱷall she would travel to Italy to ~~see~~ ∧**preview** the newest fashions⊙

CHAPTER 6

WRITING A NARRATIVE ESSAY

The **Grade 6 PSSA Writing Assessment** will be given in two sessions of 60 minutes each. The test booklet will have two writing prompts and 5 lined pages for you to write each answer. You will have to create one of three types of writings — a *narrative, informational,* or *persuasive* essay.

On the test, you will **NOT** have a choice of what type of essay to write. During each session, the writing prompt will tell you what type of essay to create. The next three chapters will look at each type of essay you may have to write for the test. This chapter will look at writing a *narrative essay.*

WHAT IS A NARRATIVE ESSAY?

To **narrate** means to "remember, recollect, or tell about an event or series of related events." A narrative essay creates, interprets, and mixes events that have really happened or might have happened. The reader is given an impression of witnessing actual events, even if the narrative is a fictional one.

Narrative writing allows someone to write in a creative fashion. It offers a writer a chance to understand his or her emotions and the emotions of others. On the **Grade 6 PSSA Writing Assessment,** the writing prompt may require you to tell about an event you saw and how people in that event reacted.

Let's take a look at a sample writing prompt for a narrative essay:

You will have one class period (but no more than 60 minutes if your class is longer) to plan, write, and proofread your response, making any necessary corrections.

Planning

- Think about what you want to write.
- Reread the prompt to make sure you are writing about the topic.
- Make notes. Use your prewriting skills, such as mapping or outlining.
- Carefully read the five statements below the prompt. Each statement refers to one of the scoreable domains: focus, content, organization, style, and conventions.

Writing

- Write your essay on the paper your teacher gives you.
- Proofread your essay and make necessary corrections.

READ THE ENTIRE PROMPT CAREFULLY.

> **One of the most enjoyable activities in life is visiting interesting places.**
>
> **Write about a visit you made and tell why it was an interesting experience.**

As you write your paper remember to:

- Describe the visit and why it was interesting.

- Use specific details to develop your narrative.

- Present your ideas in a clear and logical order, including an introduction, body, and conclusion.

- Use a variety of words and well-constructed sentences.

- Correct any errors in grammar, mechanics, spelling, usage, and sentence formation.

You may feel somewhat uncomfortable writing about your own experiences. Remember, the purpose of the test is ***not*** to find out about the details of your personal life. The **PSSA Writing Assessment** is ***not*** concerned with your actual experiences, but with your ability to write about them.

HINTS FOR
WRITING A NARRATIVE ESSAY

When you write a narrative essay, you will be scored on how well you ***focus, present content, organize, use style,*** and ***follow writing conventions*** in your answer. Let's use these five "scoreable domains" as guides to help you write this kind of essay.

FOCUS

The **focus** of your essay will be found in the directions and the first guideline of the prompt. The directions will tell you to write about some kind of experience you had or saw. In the sample writing prompt on the previous page, you are asked to write about a visit you had to an interesting place. Therefore, your first task is to:

> ***Select an experience you have had while***
> ***visiting an interesting place.***

To choose a good experience to write about, begin by first thinking about all the interesting visits you have made. You may have had an interesting visit on a family trip to a relative's house or on a field trip to a museum or ballpark.

Brainstorm as many of these experiences as you can think of. People often brainstorm in groups, but you can do the same thing on your own. When you *brainstorm,* you jot down any ideas that come into your head, even if some of them do not seem very good. Afterwards, you review the list you created to see which ideas are really good.

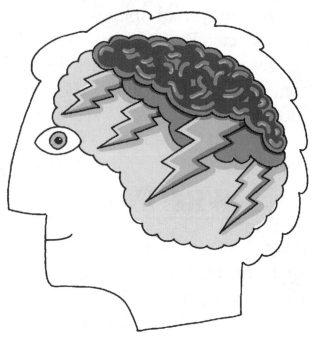

The ideas you come up with will supply the information you will need to write your essay. Now fill in the graphic that follows for the sample writing prompt.

List some interesting visits you have made.

1.

2.

3.

4.

From the list you just created, choose the visit in which you feel you had the most interesting experiences to write about:

> ***The visit in which I had the most interesting experiences was***
>
> _____

Remember: Once you choose an experience to write about, everything you write in your essay should relate in some way to that experience.

CONTENT

In a narrative essay, you will have to tell about something that has happened. You must provide ideas and details to describe and explain the event you have chosen. This content will help your reader to make a mental picture of what you are writing about.

When you describe an experience, you need to supply the ***who, what, where, when,*** and ***how.*** Think about all five senses in describing something. You should also tell how the experience you are writing about has affected you.

The ***topic map*** on the next page can help you to organize your thoughts when writing a narrative essay. It will help you to remember details of the experience you are writing about.

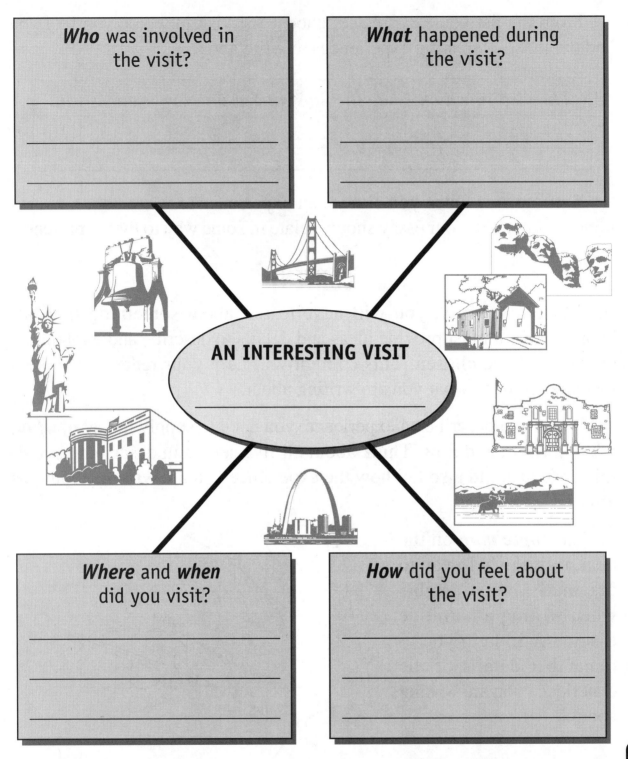

Who was involved in the visit?

_____

_____

_____

What happened during the visit?

_____

_____

_____

AN INTERESTING VISIT

_____

Where and **when** did you visit?

_____

_____

_____

How did you feel about the visit?

_____

_____

_____

The information you jot down in this topic map will become the body of your essay. Now take the visit you selected on page 53. Put that visit in the center of the topic map above. Then fill out the rest of the boxes with details about that experience.

ORGANIZATION

Be sure your essay has a clear introduction, body, and conclusion. Let's briefly review the organization of each of these parts of your answer:

INTRODUCTION

★ The introduction should identify the visit you had and have decided to write about in responding to the prompt. This introduction provides the focus for the rest of your narrative essay.

BODY

★ A narrative essay is usually organized in *time order*. You tell about an event or series of events in the order in which they happened.

★ To help you organize your writing, it may help to take your topic map on the opposite page and number the points in the order you want to introduce them in your essay.

CONCLUSION

★ You can often restate your opening statement in your conclusion.

★ You should say something about how the event you are writing about has affected you or led to important changes in your life. For example, did you learn anything important on your visit? Did it leave you with any happy memories that you still cherish?

USEFUL TRANSITION WORDS

Narrative essays are usually organized in time order. The following transition words are often useful:

★ At five o'clock, . . .

★ On Monday, . . .

★ That Summer, . . .

★ An hour later, . . .

★ The next morning, . . .

★ Next, then, finally

STYLE

You might recall that *style* includes the *voice* you use when writing and the *tone* of what you write. You create this style through the choice of words you write as well as the sentence structures you use.

Decide on the style while you plan your essay. Is your response to the prompt going to be comical, sad, serious, or argumentative? For a narrative essay, most often you will be telling about things you experienced directly. As a result, the style you use might be very informal and personal, told from you own viewpoint, using "I" or "we." For the **voice** and **tone,** let the prompt be your guide.

Remember to use vivid words that will appeal to as many of the five senses as you can to help recreate your experiences. You should also use specific words that provide plenty of information.

If the narrative you are going to write about is funny, you might try to use humorous language:

> Who could have predicted that a visit to the candy store just around the corner from my house would become the most interesting experience of my life? Then again, my life has not exactly been a model of excitement so far.

However, if your narrative is of a more serious nature or even tragic, you would need to use an entirely different tone:

> Without a doubt, it was one of the saddest moments of my life. I can still remember almost every detail about the visit to the hospital to visit Mr. Philips, our elderly neighbor. The event of that visit is still sharply carved in my mind. On that day, I experienced something I will never forget.

WRITING CONVENTIONS

After you have finished writing your essay, edit and revise your work. Check your essay for any errors in writing conventions. Be careful to avoid errors in grammar, usage, capitalization, punctuation, and spelling.

A MODEL NARRATIVE ESSAY

The essay on the next page is a sample answer that one student wrote about an interesting visit he had. As you read this essay, pay particular attention to the suggestions in the boxes alongside the essay.

This paragraph introduces the topic of the essay.

Last summer my family took a car trip to Disney World in Orlando, Florida. This visit was one of the most exciting and fun adventures of my entire life.

Florida is very different from Pennsylvania. The weather was very hot, and palm trees were everywhere. Many of the buildings and hotels were painted bright pink. The first afternoon we arrived in Florida, we took it easy. We drove to a beach and went swimming in the warm waters of the Atlantic Ocean.

These paragraphs give details about Florida and Disney World by telling who, what, when, and where of the visit.

The next day we went to Disney World. This is a vast area with several different theme parks. In the "Magic Kingdom" we shook hands with Mickey Mouse and Donald Duck. My favorite ride was the Pirates of the Caribbean. I felt a lump in my stomach as we plunged into the darkness. On the third day of our visit we went on to Epcot, where we learned how science and technology are changing our world. We also visited buildings surrounding an artificial lake, and saw people from around the world. We enjoyed eating many kinds of tasty foods from all over the world.

The last paragraph ends with a conclusion explaining why this was an interesting experience.

I have visited lots of fascinating places, but this was the most interesting visit by far. The park has interesting things appealing to all tastes. The thrilling rides, colorful cartoon characters, and the sunny weather made for many happy memories.

PRACTICE
WRITING A NARRATIVE ESSAY

Now it's your turn. Use your notes from the topic map you completed earlier in this chapter to write a narrative essay about an interesting visit you had. Remember, you can have an interesting experience visiting a place in your own neighborhood as well as somewhere far away.

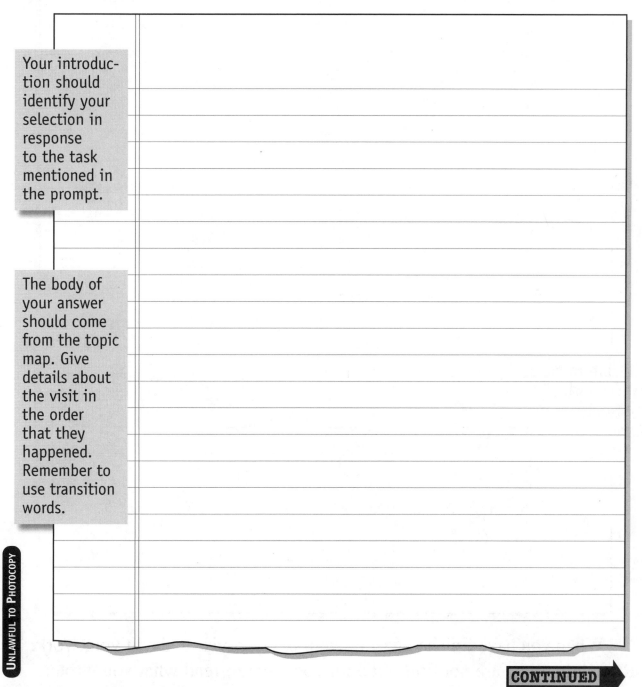

Your introduction should identify your selection in response to the task mentioned in the prompt.

The body of your answer should come from the topic map. Give details about the visit in the order that they happened. Remember to use transition words.

CONTINUED ➡

Be sure to
finish with
a strong
conclusion.

When you have finished writing your essay, revise and edit your work.
Remember, you are not finished until you have re-read what you wrote.

Practice Exercises

Directions: Read and then answer the writing prompt below:

You will have one class period (but no more than 60 minutes if your class is longer) to plan, write, and proofread your response, making any necessary corrections.

Planning

- Think about what you want to write.
- Reread the prompt to make sure you are writing about the topic.
- Make notes. Use your prewriting skills, such as mapping or outlining.
- Carefully read the five statements below the prompt. Each statement refers to one of the scoreable domains: focus, content, organization, style, and conventions.

Writing

- Write your essay on the paper your teacher gives you.
- Proofread your essay and make necessary corrections.

READ THE ENTIRE PROMPT CAREFULLY.

Sometimes we accomplish things we are proud of.

Write about a time you accomplished something you are proud of.

As you write your paper remember to:

- Tell about what you did and why you feel proud of it.

- Use specific details to develop your narrative.

- Present your ideas in a clear and logical order, including an introduction, body, and conclusion.

- Use a variety of words and well-constructed sentences.

- Correct any errors in grammar, mechanics, spelling, usage, and sentence formation.

First, list a series of accomplishments you are proud of.

1.

2.

3.

4.

Select **one** time you accomplished something that you wish to write about:

_____

Use the topic map below to supply the necessary details and examples you will need to support your essay.

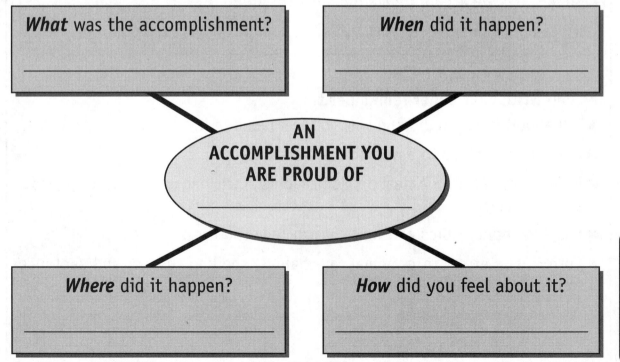

What was the accomplishment?
_____

When did it happen?
_____

AN
ACCOMPLISHMENT YOU
ARE PROUD OF
_____

Where did it happen?
_____

How did you feel about it?
_____

CONTINUED

When you have finished writing your essay, revise and edit your work.
Remember, you are not finished until you have reviewed what you wrote.

CHAPTER 7

WRITING AN INFORMATIONAL ESSAY

On the **Grade 6 PSSA Writing Assessment** you may have to write an informational essay. Let's begin by looking at what an informational essay is.

WHAT IS AN INFORMATIONAL ESSAY?

Informational writing is one of the most common forms of writing in our society. Informational writing is used by people to share knowledge and communicate messages, instructions, or ideas to others. It is used in the field of education, in business, as well as in our personal lives.

Informational writing performs a wide variety of functions in our lives:

★ It allows us to present information in written form.

★ It allows us to report, explain, direct, summarize, and define things.

★ It allows us to organize and analyze information by explaining, comparing, contrasting, and explaining cause and effect.

★ It allows us to evaluate information by judging it, ranking it, and deciding on it.

On the **Grade 6 PSSA Writing Assessment,** the writing prompt for an informational essay may ask you to *explain why* or *how something happened*. A different type of writing prompt may ask you to *give suggestions*. A third type of prompt may ask you to *describe something* or *to tell how things are different or alike*.

Let's look at what you have to do for each of these types of informational essays:

★ To *explain why* something happened, you need to identify the causes that made it happen.

★ To *explain how* something happened, you must *explain the way in which it happened*. For example, to *explain how* someone made an important decision, you need to:

   (1) *identify* the problem the person faced;

   (2) *list the choices* the person had; and

   (3) *describe the steps* the person went through in making the decision.

★ To *give suggestions,* think about what should be done in the situation described in the prompt. Then provide your *suggestions* and *explain how* or *why* each suggestion would be useful.

★ To *describe* something, tell about its qualities. For example, to *describe* a favorite place, first identify that place. Then tell about its climate, how it looks, and what you can do there.

On the following page is a sample writing prompt for an informational essay:

You will have one class period (but no more than 60 minutes if your class is longer) to plan, write, and proofread your response, making any necessary corrections.

Planning

- Think about what you want to write.
- Reread the prompt to make sure you are writing about the topic.
- Make notes. Use your prewriting skills, such as mapping or outlining.
- Carefully read the five statements below the prompt. Each statement refers to one of the scoreable domains: focus, content, organization, style, and conventions.

Writing

- Write your essay on the paper your teacher gives you.
- Proofread your essay and make necessary corrections.

READ THE ENTIRE PROMPT CAREFULLY.

Imagine your family is moving to another city and you can take only three of your own possessions along.

Write to inform your family of the three belongings you want to take and why you selected those three.

As you write your paper remember to:

- Tell what three items you would take along and why.

- Include enough information and details so that your family will understand what you want to take and why.

- Present your ideas in a clear and logical order, including an introduction, body, and conclusion.

- Use a variety of words and well-constructed sentences.

- Correct any errors in grammar, mechanics, spelling, usage, and sentence formation.

HINTS FOR WRITING AN INFORMATIONAL ESSAY

Your informational essay will receive a separate score for each of the five "scoreable domains:" *focus, content, organization, style,* and the use of *writing conventions*. Let's use these five domains as guides for creating your response.

FOCUS

The focus of your informational essay will be provided by the directions and the first guideline. These directions will tell you to *explain, describe,* or *compare,* or *suggest* something. In the sample prompt on the previous page, the directions told you to write about three items you would take with you if you moved and why you would take those particular things.

Your first task is to select the three items that you would take. One simple way of selecting these items is to jot down a list of all your most important possessions. Remember, three of these items will provide the focus of what you write. Now complete the list below.

List some of your most important possessions.

1.   4.

2.   5.

3.   6.

Select **three objects** from the list that are most important to you:

> *Three belongings that I would want to take if we moved are*
>
> 1. _____
>
> 2. _____
>
> 3. _____

Once you choose the three possessions you would take, everything you write in your essay should relate to those three objects and why you would want to take them with you.

CONTENT

In an informational essay, you have to provide details to support your main points. In the sample prompt, you have to *explain why* you would take those three particular items. This means you have to give facts and examples that show why they are important to you.

The graphic organizer below will help you to organize your thoughts. It makes it easy to come up with particular details and examples you can use to support your essay.

	What is it?	Describe it:	Why is it important to you?
(1)			
(2)			
(3)			

The information you jot down in the graphic organizer on page 69 will become the basis of your answer. Start with the first possession you chose. Write it in the box on the left. Next, describe the item in the box in the middle. Then fill out the last box with details about why it is important to you. Take a few minutes to complete the organizer, but be sure to leave enough time to write and revise your essay.

ORGANIZATION

Let's briefly review the organization of your essay:

INTRODUCTION

★ The introduction provides the focus for the rest of your informational essay. In the case of our sample writing prompt, the introduction should identify three of your most important possessions.

★ Then provide a transition to the body of your essay.

BODY

★ Organize your essay in some logical order   time, space, or order of importance. An informational essay is often organized by order of importance. You might list the most important item first. For the sample prompt, you have to list the three possessions and explain why each is important to you.

★ Begin by telling about the first possession you would take. Use separate paragraphs to describe the second and third possessions. Do not forget to fully describe the object and tell why you would take it.

CONCLUSION

★ Restate your opening statement. Then briefly summarize what the possessions are and their importance in your life.

USEFUL TRANSITION WORDS

Often an informational essay presents several points in order of importance. Some useful transition words and phrases for informational essays include:

★ The first item, the second item, the last item

★ The first reason, the second reason, the third reason

★ One way, a second way, the next way

★ In addition, another, also

STYLE

The purpose of an informational writing is to inform the reader. Therefore, the *voice* and *tone* of an informational writing should make use of precise words to give the reader a clear idea of the things being described or explained. Transition words play an especially important role in the style of an informational essay. They help the reader to follow the separate steps of an explanation or description.

WRITING CONVENTIONS

In the final step, edit and revise your work. Check your essay for any errors in grammar, usage, capitalization, punctuation, or spelling.

A MODEL INFORMATIONAL ESSAY

The essay on the next page is a sample of what one student wrote in response to the prompt. Carefully read the suggestions alongside the essay.

The introduction makes some general comments about the situation provided in the prompt. It then goes on to identify the possessions asked for in the prompt.

Here, the writer describes the first item and explains its importance.

The writer then gives facts and details about the second and third possessions.

Notice the use of the transition word "lastly" to signal the reader the final possession is being discussed.

The conclusion signals closure to the reader.

It's hard to imagine moving to another city, but this does happen. If I could select only three possessions to take along, they would not be hard to choose. My three most important possessions are my grandmother's picture, my third-grade soccer trophy, and my pet puppy.

Ever since I can remember, I can see my grandmother's picture. It was taken in 1958, when she was just married. The photo is black and white. It shows her smiling and wearing a beautiful lace wedding dress. I was very close to my grandmother before she passed away. When I see this picture, it always helps me to remember her.

My third grade trophy is another belonging I could not live without. The trophy is not much to look at. It is only 12 inches high and made of shiny plastic. The inscription says, "Most Valuable Player." It was my best soccer season. Again, I would take this object not because it is valuable, but because of the memories it holds.

Lastly, I would not move to a new city without my pet puppy, Jarry. He is a pup with light brown fur, about 6 months old. I love to watch him chew on my old shoe. Sometimes, I hold him and feel his warmth while I'm watching television or getting ready for bed. He is also my responsibility, so there is no way I could leave him behind.

It would be hard to select only three possessions. But I think I have chosen three objects that have great meaning to me as a person rather than things that cost the most. That is why my grandmother's picture, my trophy, and my pet puppy would never be left behind.

PRACTICE
WRITING AN INFORMATIONAL ESSAY

Now use your notes from the topic map you completed to write an informational essay about three possessions you would take and why you would choose them.

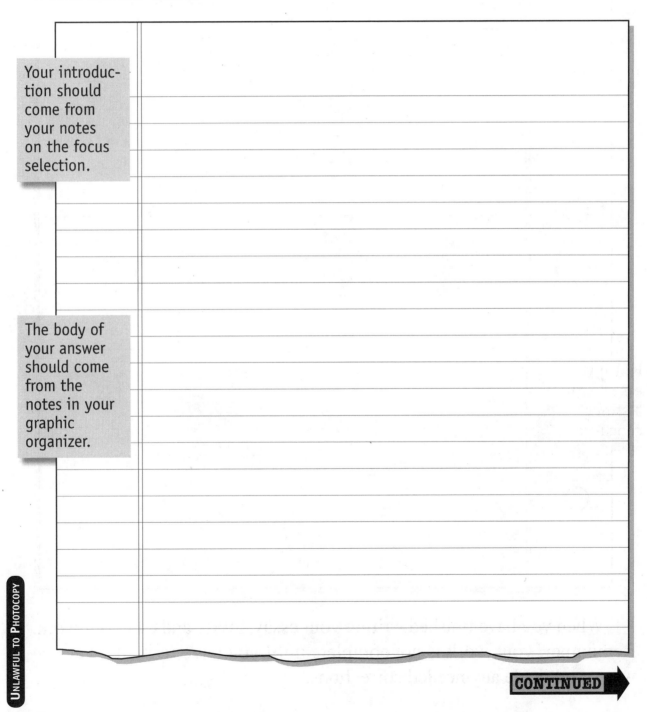

Your introduction should come from your notes on the focus selection.

The body of your answer should come from the notes in your graphic organizer.

CONTINUED ➡

Finish your essay with a strong conclusion.

When you have finished writing your essay, revise and edit your work. Remember, your work is not complete until you have re-read what you wrote and made any needed corrections.

Practice Exercises

Directions: Read and then answer the writing prompt below:

You will have one class period (but no more than 60 minutes if your class is longer) to plan, write, and proofread your response, making any necessary corrections.

Planning

- Think about what you want to write.
- Reread the prompt to make sure you are writing about the topic.
- Make notes. Use your prewriting skills, such as mapping or outlining.
- Carefully read the five statements below the prompt. Each statement refers to one of the scoreable domains: focus, content, organization, style, and conventions.

Writing

- Write your essay on the paper your teacher gives you.
- Proofread your essay and make necessary corrections.

READ THE ENTIRE PROMPT CAREFULLY.

We all have favorite things we like to study and do.

Write about your favorite subject in school and why you enjoy it.

As you write your paper remember to:

- Tell about your favorite subject and explain why you enjoy it.

- Use specific details to develop your essay.

- Present your ideas in a clear and logical order, including an introduction, body, and conclusion.

- Use a variety of words and well-constructed sentences.

- Correct any errors in grammar, mechanics, spelling, usage, and sentence formation.

Now complete the list below.

List some of your favorite subjects.

1.

2.

3.

Select **one** subject that is your favorite in school.

> ***My favorite subject in school is***
>
> _____

Use the graphic organizer below and continue on the next page to help you think of details and examples you will need to support your essay.

Identify the Subject:	Describe the Subject:

Reasons Why This Subject Is Your Favorite:
(1)
(2)
(3)

Use the blank paper on this and the next page to write your informational essay.

CONTINUED ➡

After you finish writing, revise and edit your essay. It is not complete until you have checked your work and are satisfied with it.

CHAPTER 8

WRITING A PERSUASIVE ESSAY

On the **Grade 6 PSSA Writing Assessment,** you may be asked to write a persuasive essay. Let's begin by looking at what a persuasive essay is.

WHAT IS A PERSUASIVE ESSAY?

A **persuasive essay** moves a reader to take an action, to change an opinion, or to believe something. Most often, the writer of a persuasive essay seeks to convince the reader to adopt the writer's point of view.

Knowing how to write a persuasive essay is useful for three reasons:

★ Persuasive essay writing requires you to use important thinking skills in preparing your arguments.

★ Persuasive essay writing requires you to learn how to choose a particular stand on an issue from a variety of positions.

★ Persuasive essay writing helps teach you how to state your position, support or defend it, and argue against others who might oppose your views.

Let's look at a sample prompt requiring you to write a persuasive essay.

You will have one class period (but no more than 60 minutes if your class is longer) to plan, write, and proofread your response, making any necessary corrections.

Planning

- Think about what you want to write.
- Reread the prompt to make sure you are writing about the topic.
- Make notes. Use your prewriting skills, such as mapping or outlining.
- Carefully read the five statements below the prompt. Each statement refers to one of the scoreable domains: focus, content, organization, style, and conventions.

Writing

- Write your essay on the paper your teacher gives you.
- Proofread your essay and make necessary corrections.

READ THE ENTIRE PROMPT CAREFULLY.

Your school is considering inviting a fast-food restaurant to provide school lunches.

Write to persuade the principal that your school either should or should not invite a fast-food restaurant to provide school lunches to students.

As you write your paper remember to:

- Clearly state your position on serving fast-food lunches to students.

- Include specific facts, details, reasons, to convince the principal of your position on the issue of serving fast-food to students in school.

- Present your ideas in a clear and logical order, including an introduction, body, and conclusion.

- Use a variety of words and well-constructed sentences.

- Correct any errors in grammar, mechanics, spelling, usage, and sentence formation.

HINTS FOR WRITING A PERSUASIVE ESSAY

As with narrative and informational essays, your persuasive essay will receive a separate score on each of the five "scoreable domains" *focus, content, organization, style,* and the use of *writing conventions.*

FOCUS

The **focus** of your essay will be provided by the directions and the first guideline of the prompt. The prompt will ask you to take a position on some question or issue. For example, the sample prompt on the previous page asks you to take a stand on whether your school should invite a fast-food restaurant to provide school lunches. Should your school serve fast-food lunches or not?

Your first task is to decide what position to take on the issue presented in the prompt. One way to decide what position to take is to make a list of your reasons in favor of each side. Try to think of all the advantages that would occur if either position were adopted. Also think of the disadvantages of each position.

In Favor of Fast-food School Lunches	Opposed to Fast-food School Lunches
1. Students enjoy fast foods and will eat more of their lunches.	1. Fast food is not very healthy for students.
2. Some parents do not have time to prepare lunch for their children.	2. Having fast food in school sets the wrong example for many students.
3. Now you add a reason: _____	3. Now you add a reason: _____
_____	_____
_____	_____

Once you have completed your list of reasons for each side of the issue, you have to select your **position.** You will state your position in the introduction of your essay. Your position is the side of the issue that you support. It will serve as the focus of your persuasive essay.

Select the position you support on the issue of serving fast-food lunches in school.

My position is _____

CONTENT

Now you have to support your position with reasons. Stay focused on providing reasons that support your side of the issue. *You should only give the reasons for your own side. Never give the reasons for both sides of an issue in a persuasive essay.* Remember, you are trying to convince the reader to adopt your point of view on this issue.

Each reason that you present in your essay should be explained with examples and facts. After a person reads your essay, he or she should come away believing that your point of view is correct. For example, if you believe your school should serve fast-food lunches, you want to convince your reader to adopt the same point of view. You might point out that many of your friends enjoy fast foods and would probably eat more of their lunch if fast foods were served.

ORGANIZATION

Like the other types of essays, a persuasive essay needs an introduction, body, and conclusion. Let's briefly review the organization of each part to see the role it plays in helping you to argue your position.

INTRODUCTION

★ The introduction should clearly state to the reader your position on the issue in the prompt.

★ There are many ways to follow the opening statement of your position. One common approach is to briefly state each reason why you favor the position you have taken. These reasons are then more fully discussed in the body of your essay.

BODY

★ In the body of your essay, give the reasons for your position together with supporting details.

★ Writers often present their reasons in *order of importance*. You can start with your most important reason first. Another way is to start with the least important reason and end with the most important reason.

★ Use a separate paragraph for each reason you present. The focus of each paragraph should be a discussion of that particular reason.

CONCLUSION

ur essay by restating your position on the issue. le prompt, you would restate whether you favor t-food school lunches.

tive in your conclusion. For example, you may want with a challenging question that summarizes your could also briefly summarize the reasons why you right.

USEFUL TRANSITION WORDS

For a persuasive essay, some useful transition words and phrases include:

★ First, second, third

★ Therefore, one can see

★ In conclusion, I feel

★ The first reason, the second reason, the third reason

STYLE

Probably in the past few days you have tried to persuade someone — a parent, friend, or teacher. You may have attempted to borrow something, or tried to persuade someone to allow you to go somewhere or do something. How successful were you in presenting your viewpoint?

Good persuaders try to convince others to accept their ideas or adopt their points of view, usually relying on *reasons* and *facts* to be convincing. When you write your persuasive essay, let the prompt guide you in choosing the right *voice* and *tone* that would best match your **audience** and **purpose.**

Writers sometimes adopt a neutral or unbiased tone. The writer avoids references to himself or herself, so that the writer's opinions appear to be impartial.

On occasion, however, a persuasive writer will appeal to emotions. Most often, this happens when the writer is outraged by the situation or believes the other side is morally wrong.

WRITING CONVENTIONS

As always, edit and revise your work after you finish writing. Check for errors you may have made in grammar, usage, capitalization, punctuation, and spelling.

A MODEL PERSUASIVE ESSAY

The essay on the next page is one student's response to whether his school should provide fast-food lunches to students. As you read this essay be mindful of the logical manner in which the writer presents his arguments.

This introduction states his position and gives a preview of the reasons why.

Here the author previews the main reasons for his position.

My school is considering inviting a fast-food restaurant like McDonalds or Taco Bell to provide school lunches. I oppose fast-food lunches in school. First, fast food is unhealthy. Second, fast-food lunches in school may set a bad example for students. Third, fast food lunches would add to the litter problem in our school.

In the body of the essay, the writer discusses each reason in a separate paragraph with supporting details.

The most important reason why I oppose fast-food lunches in school is because fast foods are unhealthy. Fast foods have a lot of fat and salt in them. They are often fried in fat. All of this is unhealthy.

The second reason why I oppose fast-food lunches is that they set a bad example. Kids often get hooked on fast foods and never learn to appreciate healthy, well-balanced meals. Schools should not encourage this behavior.

The final reason I oppose fast-food lunches in school is that they will create too much litter. Students will throw their wrappers and soda cups on the floor. Garbage cans will quickly overflow with all of this added litter.

In conclusion, there are three good reasons why we should not allow our school to serve fast-food lunches. It would be unhealthy, it would set a bad example for students, and it would create a litter problem.

The conclusion summarizes the writer's point of view.

PRACTICE
WRITING A PERSUASIVE ESSAY

Use your notes to write a persuasive essay for or against fast-food lunches in school.

State your position. Then preview the reasons for it or make a general statement about fast-food lunches.

Explain the reasons for your position in detail. Use a separate paragraph for each reason you present. Remember, you are trying to convince your reader to adopt your point of view.

CONTINUED ➡

Summarize your point of view in your conclusion or provide some other strong persuasive finish.

When you have completed writing your essay, revise and edit your work. Remember, you are not finished until you have re-read what you wrote and have made any needed corrections.

Practice Exercises

Directions: Read and then answer the writing prompt below:

You will have one class period (but no more than 60 minutes if your class is longer) to plan, write, and proofread your response, making any necessary corrections.

Planning

■ Think about what you want to write.
■ Reread the prompt to make sure you are writing about the topic.
■ Make notes. Use your prewriting skills, such as mapping or outlining.
■ Carefully read the five statements below the prompt. Each statement refers to one of the scoreable domains: focus, content, organization, style, and conventions.

Writing

■ Write your essay on the paper your teacher gives you.
■ Proofread your essay and make necessary corrections.

READ THE ENTIRE PROMPT CAREFULLY.

Some teachers give homework on weekends, while other teachers feel that weekends should be for family activities and relaxation.

Write to persuade school officials to accept your views on whether sixth graders should be assigned homework on the weekends.

As you write your paper remember to:

■ Clearly state your position on whether or not homework should be assigned on weekends.

■ Include specific facts, details, reasons, to convince the school officials to accept your position on the issue of having homework over the weekend.

■ Present your ideas in a clear and logical order, including an introduction, body, and conclusion.

■ Use a variety of words and well-constructed sentences.

■ Correct any errors in grammar, mechanics, spelling, usage, and sentence formation.

Try to think of all the advantages and disadvantages if either position were adopted. Use the boxes below and on the next page to supply the reasons you will need to support your essay.

In Favor of Homework on Weekends

1. Reason: _____

   _____

2. Reason: _____

   _____

3. Reason: _____

   _____

Opposed to Homework on Weekends

1. Reason: _____

   _____

2. Reason: _____

   _____

3. Reason: _____

   _____

Now that you have created a list of reasons in favor of each side of the issue, you have to select your position.

> ### *Select the position you support on the issue of homework on the weekends.*
>
> *My position is* _____

Use the blank paper below and on the next page to write your persuasive essay.

CONTINUED →

When you have completed your essay, you should revise and edit it.
After you have checked your essay and are satisfied with it, you are finished.

UNIT 4:

A PRACTICE WRITING TEST

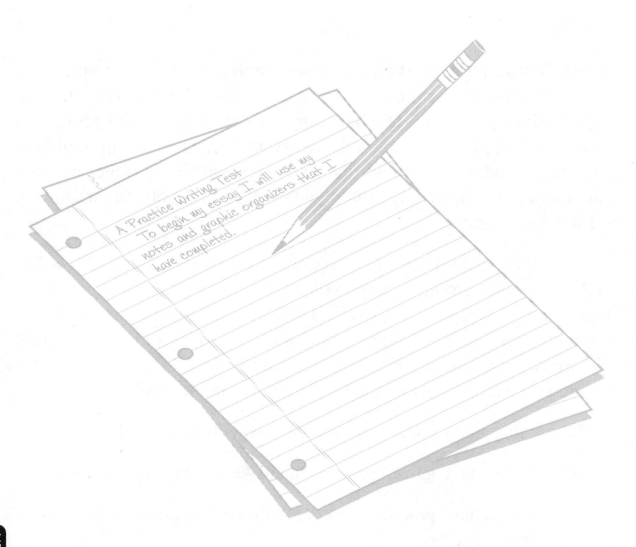

A Practice Writing Test
    To begin my essay I will use my
notes and graphic organizers that I
have completed.

CHAPTER 9

A PRACTICE GRADE 6 PSSA WRITING ASSESSMENT

On the **Grade 6 PSSA Writing Assessment,** you will be required to respond to **two** writing prompts. They will be of different types. During each session, you will **NOT** have any choice about which prompt to answer or type of writing to complete. However, each prompt will give you some freedom to select your own ideas within its directions and guidelines. For each writing prompt, you will be given 60 minutes to plan and write your answer.

Unlike the actual test, the practice writing test that follows has **THREE** writing prompts. Since you are taking this test as practice, we suggest that you respond to **ALL THREE** writing prompts. Take each one during a separate 60 minute session. **DO NOT** look at the prompt until you are about to take that part of the practice test. Do all of your pre-writing and final drafting on the lines provided in this book.

Taking this practice test will provide you with several advantages:

★ You will have gained practice in answering each type of prompt.

★ You will have practice working within a 60-minute time requirement.

PROMPT #1: A NARRATIVE ESSAY

You will have one class period (but no more than 60 minutes if your class is longer) to plan, write, and proofread your response, making any necessary corrections.

Planning

- Think about what you want to write.
- Reread the prompt to make sure you are writing about the topic.
- Make notes. Use your prewriting skills, such as mapping or outlining.
- Carefully read the five statements below the prompt. Each statement refers to one of the scoreable domains: focus, content, organization, style, and conventions.

Writing

- Write your essay on the paper your teacher gives you.
- Proofread your essay and make necessary corrections.

READ THE ENTIRE PROMPT CAREFULLY.

Life is filled with various celebrations.

Write about a time you enjoyed a celebration with your family or friends.

As you write your paper remember to:

- Write about what you celebrated, and how you felt about it
- Use specific details to develop your narrative.
- Present your ideas in a clear and logical order, including an introduction, body, and conclusion.
- Use a variety of words and well-constructed sentences.
- Correct any errors in grammar, mechanics, spelling, usage, and sentence formation.

PLANNING YOUR ANSWER

The *planning stage* is where you come up with ideas for what you are going to write in your essay. You have learned about several different graphic organizers that are available to plan your answer. Use the hamburger outline below *or* the blank on the following page for whatever other pre-writing format you prefer to plan your essay.

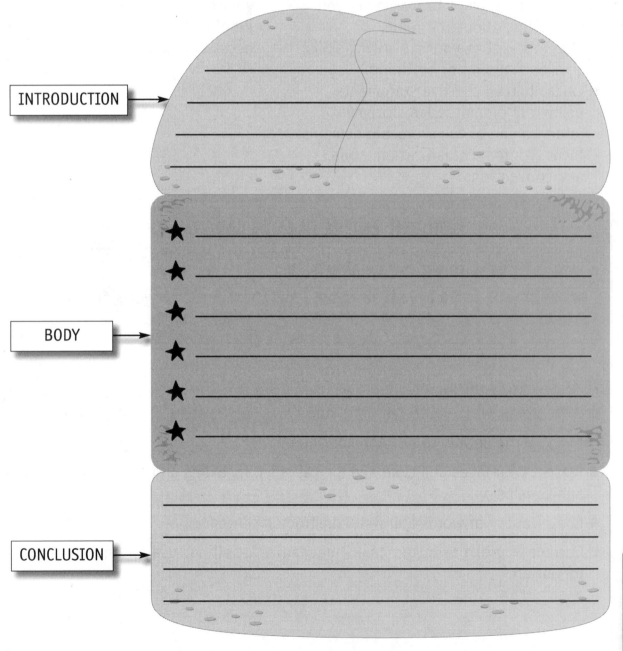

INTRODUCTION

BODY

CONCLUSION

SOME OTHER PREWRITING FORMAT

FIRST DRAFT

Use the space below to write your first draft.

FINAL, EDITED VERSION

Use the space below to write your final, edited version.

CONTINUED ➤

STOP

PROMPT #2: AN INFORMATIVE ESSAY

You will have one class period (but no more than 60 minutes if your class is longer) to plan, write, and proofread your response, making any necessary corrections.

Planning

- Think about what you want to write.
- Reread the prompt to make sure you are writing about the topic.
- Make notes. Use your prewriting skills, such as mapping or outlining.
- Carefully read the five statements below the prompt. Each statement refers to one of the scoreable domains: focus, content, organization, style, and conventions.

Writing

- Write your essay on the paper your teacher gives you.
- Proofread your essay and make necessary corrections.

READ THE ENTIRE PROMPT CAREFULLY.

Water is one of our most precious resources.

Write to inform a friend about how water is important to all of us and how we can protect this precious resource.

As you write your paper remember to:

- Write about why water is so important to all of us and how we can protect this precious resource.

- Include specific facts, details, reasons that would explain why water is such an important resource for all of us.

- Present your ideas in a clear and logical order, including an introduction, body, and conclusion.

- Use a variety of words and well-constructed sentences.

- Correct any errors in grammar, mechanics, spelling, usage, and sentence formation.

PLANNING YOUR ANSWER

The ***planning stage*** is where you come up with ideas for what you are going to write in your essay. You have learned about several different graphic organizers that are available to plan your answer. Use the hamburger outline below *or* the blank on the following page for whatever other pre-writing format you prefer to plan your essay.

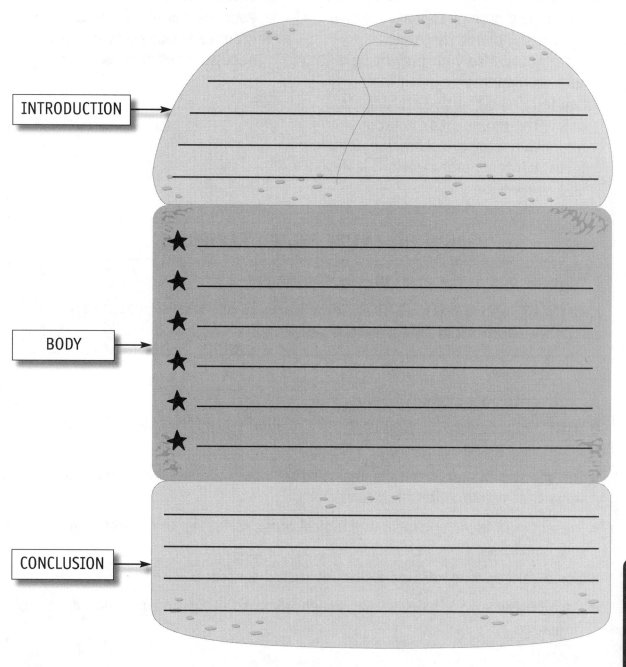

INTRODUCTION

BODY

CONCLUSION

SOME OTHER PREWRITING FORMAT

FIRST DRAFT

Use the space below to write your first draft.

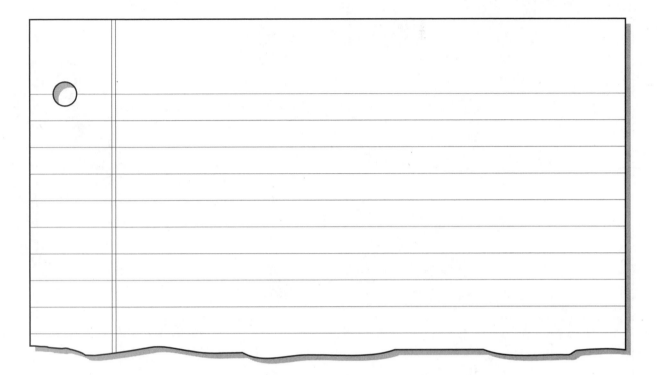

FINAL, EDITED VERSION

Use the space below to write your final, edited version.

CONTINUED ➡

STOP

PROMPT #3: A PERSUASIVE ESSAY

You will have one class period (but no more than 60 minutes if your class is longer) to plan, write, and proofread your response, making any necessary corrections.

Planning

- Think about what you want to write.
- Reread the prompt to make sure you are writing about the topic.
- Make notes. Use your prewriting skills, such as mapping or outlining.
- Carefully read the five statements below the prompt. Each statement refers to one of the scoreable domains: focus, content, organization, style, and conventions.

Writing

- Write your essay on the paper your teacher gives you.
- Proofread your essay and make necessary corrections.

READ THE ENTIRE PROMPT CAREFULLY.

Some parents allow their sixth graders to watch television during the week, while other parents allow television only on weekends.

Write to persuade someone that sixth graders either should or should not be allowed to watch television on school days.

As you write your paper remember to:

- Clearly state your position on why sixth graders should or should not be allowed to watch television on school days.

- Include specific facts, details, reasons that would convince someone of your position.

- Present your ideas in a clear and logical order, including an introduction, body, and conclusion.

- Use a variety of words and well-constructed sentences.

- Correct any errors in grammar, mechanics, spelling, usage, and sentence formation.

PLANNING YOUR ANSWER

The *planning stage* is where you come up with ideas for what you are going to write in your essay. You have learned about several different graphic organizers that are available to plan your answer. Use the hamburger outline below *or* the blank on the following page for whatever other pre-writing format you prefer to plan your essay.

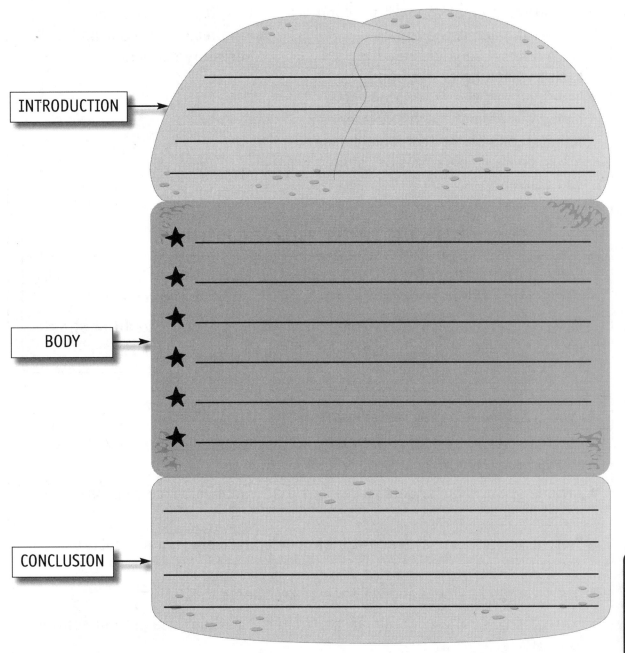

INTRODUCTION

BODY

CONCLUSION

SOME OTHER PREWRITING FORMAT

FIRST DRAFT

Use the space below to write your first draft.

FINAL, EDITED VERSION

Use the space below to write your final, edited version.

CONTINUED ➡

STOP

NOTES

NOTES